BRIDGING THE GAP

BETWEEN THE SCHOOL MEDIA SPECIALIST & THE CLASSROOM TEACHER

Written and Illustrated by Jan Grubb Philpot

ISBN 0-86530-071-2

Table of Contents

BULLETIN BOARDS THAT COMMUNICATE

GOOD FOR YOUR CLASS!

'SPECIALLY FOR YOU!

PREFACE

This book is a collection of forms, certificates, awards and more to enhance communication and positive relationships between the library media specialist and the classroom teacher. Each individual has his or her role to fill in the educational "machine"; however, unless there is effective communication, the "machine" will not be nearly as effective. The wide variety of materials in this book will provide you, the media specialist, with positive public relations tools and communication aids to promote library enthusiasm and establish a successful working relationship with your school's staff.

Each of the six chapters in this book is prefaced with a "how to" page giving you specific instructions and suggestions for using the materials within the chapter. All of the materials have been designed for instant, quick-and-easy use. Most are ready to reproduce and use now. Some require moderate construction (bulletin boards and cards). Together, these six chapters provide you with attractive "communicators" that will literally "bridge the gap" between the library/media center and the classroom. Remember, with effective communication comes understanding, and with understanding comes good will!

Jan Grubb Philpot

The Library A LOVELY Place To Visit

getting the WORD out!

FORMS FOR KEEPING
TEACHERS AND THEIR
CLASSES INFORMED OF
LIBRARY NEWS AND
MATERIALS

HOW TO USE
"GETTING THE WORD OUT!"

Newsletter Headings

Newsletters (weekly or monthly) are an excellent way to keep the school informed of library happenings. Use the newsletter headings in this section to catch teachers' attention and make them want to read on to find out about classes that have received awards, new magazines, skills being stressed for each grade level, available library services, and more. Simply paste a heading at the top of your newsletter and reproduce copies. There's no "file 13" for these eye-catching winners!

Bibliography Forms

Eye-catching bibliographies will arouse more interest than ordinary bibliographies typed on plain paper. Use the forms in this section to provide teachers with requested bibliographies for specific topics as well as fun seasonal bibliographies! If you have access to a computer, use the forms as cover sheets for prepared bibliographies.

Available Materials Forms

Every teacher will appreciate being kept informed of available library/media center materials such as new items, newspapers and magazines, professional materials, equipment, and topics listed in the vertical file. Post these forms on a bulletin board or in the teachers' lounge and distribute them to individual teachers.

Note Paper

Finally — note paper designed especially for the library/media center! These specialized notes are perfect for sending messages to teachers, students, and even parents!

BRANCH OUT ...READ!

POP
in the
LIBRARY!
(and see what's new)

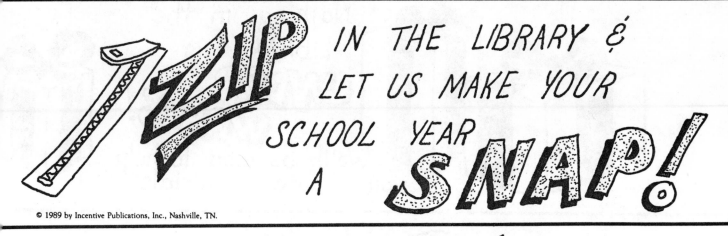

ZIP IN THE LIBRARY & LET US MAKE YOUR SCHOOL YEAR A SNAP!

TREE-mendous season for reading!

READ for a spell!

PLENTY of materials in YOUR library!

Nothing in the LIBRARY is UNDER WRAPS! We'll be glad to help you locate materials.

The Library A LOVELY Place To Visit

"BREAK" out the books!

FOWLED up on research? DUCK in the LIBRARY!

BUG OFF (to the LIBRARY!)

HUNG UP ON READING? Visit your LIBRARY!

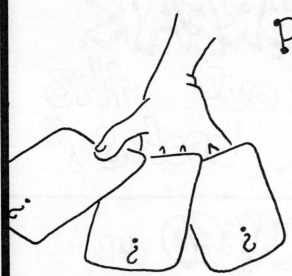

PICK A SUBJECT... ANY SUBJECT!

YOU REQUESTED A BIBLIOGRAPHY ON THE FOLLOWING TOPIC:

_____

HERE IT IS!

CALL NUMBER

TITLE

A **SPOOK-TACULAR** HALLOWEEN BIBLIOGRAPHY

MATERIALS TO BE "FIEND" IN YOUR **LIBRARY!**

I HOPE THE SPIRIT MOVES YOU TO CHECK THESE OUT!

CALL NUMBER   TITLE

YOUR EYES **FEAST** ON THESE MATERIALS!

A THANKSGIVING BIBLIOGRAPHY

call number   title

TAKE STOCK-ING OF WHAT'S IN YOUR LIBRARY!

A CHRISTMAS BIBLIOGRAPHY

CALL NUMBER   TITLE

TAKE THESE BOOKS to HEART! (You'll love them!)

A VALENTINE'S DAY BIBLIOGRAPHY

call number   title

PLENTY

OF BUNNY
TALES IN YOUR
LIBRARY!

AN EASTER BIBLIOGRAPHY

call number   title

LOOK WHAT'S NEW UNDER THE SUN!

NEW MATERIALS in the LIBRARY

call number   title

STRICTLY PROFESSIONAL

PROFESSIONAL MATERIALS IN YOUR LIBRARY

call number   title

WE'RE IN THE ...

KNOW!

with these magazines and newspapers in the LIBRARY!

title   frequency

WE'RE FULLY EQUIPPED!

AVAILABLE EQUIPMENT IN YOUR LIBRARY/ MEDIA CENTER

VERTICAL FILE

INFORMATION AVAILABLE ON THE FOLLOWING TOPICS:

SUPER SCOOP
from the library

JUST POPPING IN

with a message from your library!

A-PEELING NEWS
from your library

A MESSAGE FROM THE LIBRARY...

A message to: from: THE LIBRARY

NEWS THAT CAN "BEAR"-LY WAIT...

a message from your library!

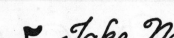

Take Note... of this news from the Library...

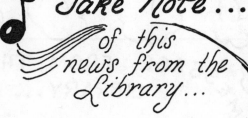

A message from your librarian...

FORMS TO AID TEACHERS IN USING THE
LIBRARY/MEDIA CENTER

HOW TO USE
"AT YOUR SERVICE!"

Teacher Request Forms

Prepare a folder of teacher request forms for each teacher. Distribute them with the media center services forms at the beginning of the year. Teachers will appreciate the simplicity of filling in a "made-to-order" form; you will appreciate having an easy, organized system for filling requests!

Follow-up Forms

Once a request has been made, give the appropriate follow-up form to the teacher to let her or him know you've taken the appropriate measures to fill the request.

Media Center Services Form

List all of the services provided by your media center on this attractive form and give a copy of it to each teacher at the beginning of the school year. This will alert teachers to the equipment and capabilities of the center and allow them to take full advantage of the center during the year.

TEACHER REQUEST FOR LIBRARY/MEDIA CENTER PURCHASES

1. I would like to request _____ (type of material) on the following topic: _____ .

2. I have examined or seen advertised the following material and would like to have it in our library/media center.

Type of material	Title (and author if applicable)	Publisher/ Producer	Catalog/ Page No.	Price

_____
Teacher

_____
Date

The following material which you requested for library purchase has been ordered:

_____

_____

I will let you know when it has arrived and has been processed.

The following material which you recommended for library purchase has arrived and has been processed. You may check it out at any time.

_____

_____

TEACHER REQUEST FORM

To the librarian:

1. Please tell stories or folk tales from _____ (country class is studying) during my class's library period on _____ _____ (date).

2. Please have a display of books and materials about _____ _____ (topic or country class is studying) available for my class to browse through and check out during their library period on _____ (date).

3. Please have a special library skills lesson or reference lesson on _____ _____ by _____ (date).

4. I would like to request an extra library period for my class the week of _____ for the purpose of _____ _____ .

5. Please send the following material(s) on the following topic(s) to my room on _____ (date).

    _____

    _____

    _____

6. Other requests: _____

    _____

    _____

    _____
    Teacher

*   This form is only for special requests; otherwise, the librarian will follow a planned schedule.

© 1989 by Incentive Publications, Inc., Nashville, TN.

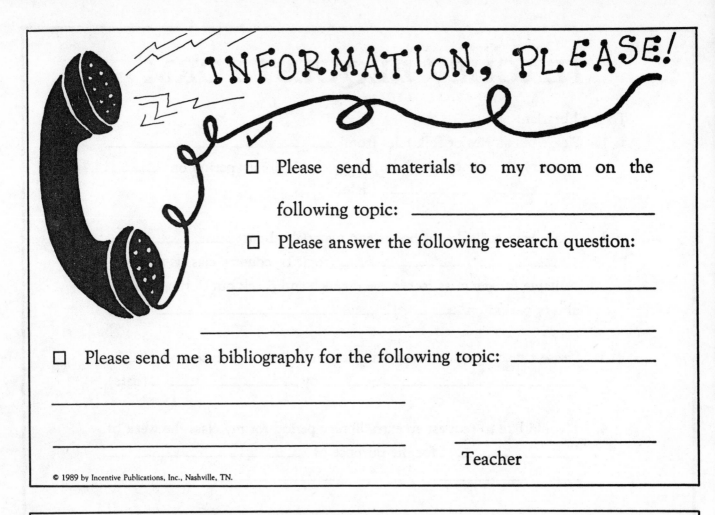

INFORMATION, PLEASE!

☐ Please send materials to my room on the

following topic: _____

☐ Please answer the following research question:

_____

_____

☐ Please send me a bibliography for the following topic: _____

_____

_____   Teacher

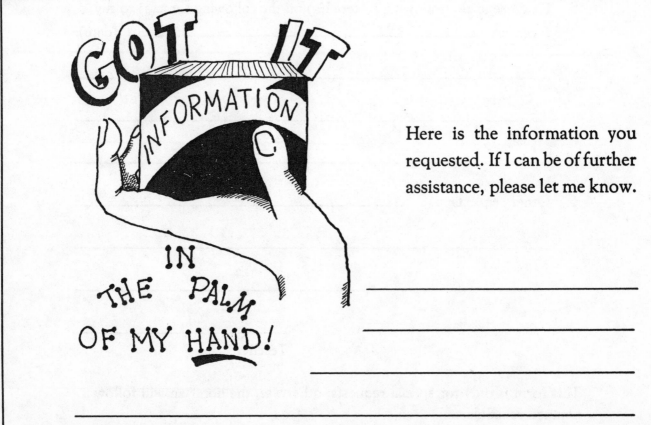

GOT IT INFORMATION IN THE PALM OF MY HAND!

Here is the information you requested. If I can be of further assistance, please let me know.

_____

_____

_____

RESERVATION REQUEST

☐ Please reserve the following date and time for my class to use the library: _____

☐ Please reserve the following books/materials: _____

_____

_____

_____
Teacher

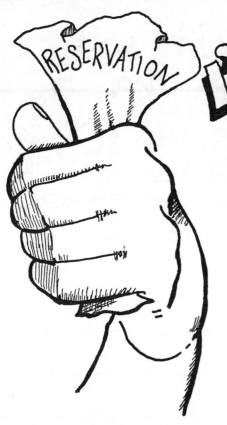

I'VE GOT IT ON HOLD!

☐ The following date and time is reserved for your class:

_____

☐ The books/materials which you requested have been reserved and may be found _____

_____ .

Need help Creating...

Please aid in the creation of the following instructional material: _____

_____

I need: ☐ a transparency   ☐ drymounting

☐ lamination   ☐ other _____

_____
Teacher

Thought you might like a SNEAK PEEK at this new material!

_____

_____

_____

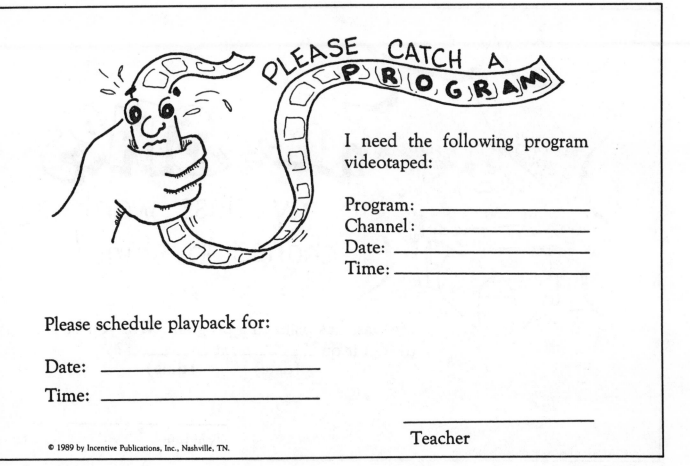

PLEASE CATCH A PROGRAM

I need the following program videotaped:

Program: _____
Channel: _____
Date: _____
Time: _____

Please schedule playback for:

Date: _____

Time: _____

_____
Teacher

CONFIRMED

The program you requested has been videotaped and will be played back on channel ____ ,

_____ at _____ .
(date)   (time)

The STARS in my class want a chance to shine!

My class has planned a program. Will you be able to film it on _____ at _____ ?
                                  (date)   (time)

_____
Teacher

BE GLAD TO CATCH YOUR STARS IN ACTION!

FILMING CONFIRMATION:

Date: _____

Time: _____

AV NEEDED!

Please send the following equipment: _____
Date: _____
Time: _____

Please send the following software: _____
Date: _____
Time: _____

_____
Teacher

The audio-visual ☐ software   you requested
☐ hardware

for _____ has been ☐ reserved.
    date   ☐ is currently unavailable.

☐ It will be delivered to your room on _____ at _____.
                                          date   time

☐ It will be available again on _____.
                                    date

LET ME AID YOU!

SERVICES PROVIDED BY YOUR MEDIA CENTER

1. _____

2. _____

3. _____

4. _____

5. _____

6. _____

7. _____

8. _____

9. _____

10. _____

11. _____

12. _____

13. _____

14. _____

15. _____

TAKING CARE OF BUSINESS

FORMS TO HELP TEACHERS "KEEP TRACK" OF
WHAT'S GOING ON IN THE LIBRARY

HOW TO USE
"TAKING CARE OF BUSINESS"

Library Schedules

The library schedules in this section will help teachers (and you!) keep track of who is supposed to be in the library when! Suggest to the teachers that they post their schedules in the classroom for reminders.

Overdue Forms

These two attractive forms will help to simplify the constant task of reminding teachers of their students' and their own overdue books and materials.

Library/Research Skills Notice and Record

Use the library/research skills notice to inform each teacher of the specific skill being reinforced during her or his class's library period. Keep a library/research skills record for each class and reproduce the records periodically (each week, month or term) for distribution to the teachers.

Library Enrichment Activities Record

This form keeps teachers abreast of what you're doing with their classes in the library each month or grading period. It will help to keep teachers from duplicating stories or audio-visual materials and it will let them know that you, too, are on your toes!

Videotape Record

Use this form when videotaping class "productions" or events. Keep a copy for your own reference and give a copy to the teacher.

Library Evaluation/Needs Survey

This survey will help you to run the best library possible by finding out what areas need work and what specific needs teachers have. Teachers will appreciate the opportunity to share their comments and ideas!

LIBRARY TIME

Your library period this year is on _____ at _____.

OPEN LIBRARY

Feel free to use the library at these times for additional research.

Day	Time

LIBRARY SCHEDULE

(school year)

TIME	MONDAY	TUESDAY	WEDNESDAY	THURSDAY	FRIDAY

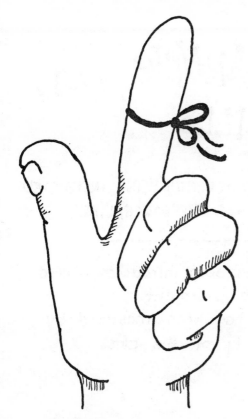

Reminding you - it's
OVERDUE

Teacher: _____

These students have overdue library books/materials. Please remind them to return the books/materials as soon as possible.

STUDENT	TITLE
_____	_____
_____	_____
_____	_____
_____	_____

I know it's hard for you- to grab a minute!

Teacher: _____

If you are no longer using the following book(s)/material(s), please return it (them) to the library as soon as possible. Thank you!

_____

_____

WE'RE LEARNING OUR SKILLS

YOUR CLASS IS CURRENTLY BEING INSTRUCTED IN THE FOLLOWING RESEARCH/LIBRARY SKILL: _____.

☐ The skill has been introduced & needs classroom reinforcement.

☐ The skill has been mastered by the majority of the class.

NEED TO SHARPEN THOSE SKILLS?

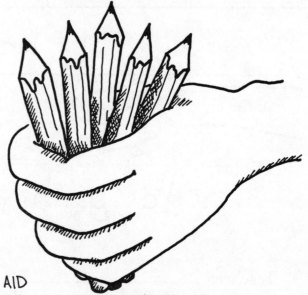

THE FOLLOWING MATERIALS ARE AVAILABLE IN THE LIBRARY TO AID IN THE TEACHING/REINFORCEMENT OF THE LIBRARY/RESEARCH SKILL _____:

_____

_____

_____

RECORD OF LIBRARY/ RESEARCH SKILLS

Teacher: _____

Grade: _____

Code:
I - introduced
R - reinforced
M - mastered

DATE	SKILL	I	R	M

RECORD OF LIBRARY
ENRICHMENT ACTIVITIES

Teacher: _____ Class: _____ Month: _____

Library Skills Activities: _____

_____

_____

Storytelling: _____

_____

_____

Books Read Aloud: _____

_____

_____

Audio-visual Materials (16 mm films, filmstrips, records, videotapes, etc.): _____

_____

_____

Other Activities: _____

_____

_____

Awards   Quiet Class Awards: _____

          Book Return Certificates: _____

          Neat and Tidy Awards: _____

_____

Comments/Suggestions For Classroom Follow-up/Etc.: _____

_____

_____

VIDEOTAPE RECORD

Call No.: _____   Class: _____
Date: _____   Title: _____

Students on camera	Characters/Roles

Students behind the scenes	Functions

LIBRARY EVALUATION/ NEEDS SURVEY

Teacher: _____

Circle the appropriate rating for each statement.

	Fair		Good		Excellent
1. I am kept informed of new library materials.	1	2	3	4	5
2. I am kept informed of skills taught to my class.	1	2	3	4	5
3. I am assisted with equipment operation.	1	2	3	4	5
4. I am aided in the creation of materials. (eg: transparencies)	1	2	3	4	5
5. Bibliographies are prepared promptly upon request.	1	2	3	4	5
6. I am kept informed of library services.	1	2	3	4	5
7. I am assisted in the location of materials.	1	2	3	4	5
8. My students are assisted in the location of materials.	1	2	3	4	5
9. I am asked for suggestions regarding library purchases.	1	2	3	4	5
10. There is sufficient open library time for additional research and other uses.	1	2	3	4	5
11. The library collection is balanced and adequate for the needs of my students and myself.	1	2	3	4	5
12. I am kept informed of library policies.	1	2	3	4	5

Additional comments:

BULLETIN BOARDS TO MAKE
TEACHERS AWARE OF LIBRARY
SERVICES AND MEDIA

HOW TO USE "BULLETIN BOARDS THAT COMMUNICATE"

The bulletin boards in this section have been designed to make teachers aware of library services and media. Good locations for display include the teachers' lounge and audio-visual production area. All of the bulletin boards can be adapted to meet information needs of students, as well.

To construct the bulletin boards in this section, you will need the following materials:

- construction paper of assorted colors
- scissors
- stapler
- tape
- glue
- crayons & markers
- gold glitter
- cotton balls
- green yarn
- fabric or patterned Contact paper
- corrugated "brick" paper or "brick" Contact paper
- 3 stockings (socks)
- 2 gloves

Objective:
  To make staff and students aware of new materials.

Hints:
  - Staple construction paper grass below the eggshells.
  - Make the eggshells three-dimensional by cutting, folding and stapling as shown.

1. Cut along the dotted lines.

2. Overlap the cut edges causing egg to bow out.

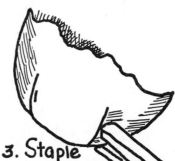

3. Staple overlapped edges. Fill shell with book jackets!

Objective:

To make teachers aware of good read-aloud books. (All books are not good read-aloud material. Examples of good read-aloud books are *How to Eat Fried Worms*, *Charlotte's Web*, and *Charlie and the Chocolate Factory*.)

Hints:

- Use fabric or patterned Contact paper to make "curtains."
- Write book titles on construction paper soup bowls.
- Use cotton balls for "snow" (outside window).

Optional Caption: SOUP-ER BOOKS FOR WINTER READING!

Objective:
  To keep staff aware of special library services.

Hint:
  ● Use green yarn for "vines."

Optional
Captions: PATCH UP YOUR RESEARCH WITH THESE
              REFERENCE BOOKS

                          or

          THESE STUDENTS ARE PUMP-IN
          UP THEIR READING HABITS

ED   BETTY   TOM   JASON   HEATHER

Objective:

To keep staff aware of materials on the professional shelf.

Hint:

- Use corrugated "brick" paper or "brick" Contact paper.
- Use real stockings. Print titles on slips of paper to be slipped in the tops of the stockings.

Optional
Captions: GET HUNG UP ON FICTION
GET HUNG UP ON NONFICTION
GET HUNG UP ON BIOGRAPHY

Objective:
To remind staff to reserve materials.

Hint:
- Stuff real gloves with tissue and staple them to the board.

Optional Caption: RESEARCH IS HEART-LY A CHORE
When you use the Reference
Section!

Objective:
To make staff and students aware of available media and services.

Hint:
- "Weave" a cornucopia!

① Cut out a brown cornucopia.

② Cut slits along dotted lines, but NOT to edge.

③ Weave <u>over</u> <u>and</u> <u>under</u> slits with paper strips (yellow). Every other strip will be woven opposite.

④ Trim edges of strips to match edges of cornucopia and glue down.

Optional Caption:
PLENTY OF NEW BOOKS

(Fill cornucopia with book jackets.)

Objective:

To aquaint faculty and students with the library staff.

Hint:

- Take photographs of each member of the library staff and glue them on musical "notes" made out of construction paper.

Optional idea: Write services provided by the library on the notes.

Objective:
   To encourage and reward proper library etiquette. (*See the section "Good for your class!")

Hints:
  ● Write the names of teachers whose classes have won awards on the lines of the book.
  ● Cover the trophy with gold glitter.

Optional ideas: Announce names of students doing especially well in learning library skills *or* post names of students who have read and reported on a specified number of books.

**AWARDS TO ENCOURAGE STUDENTS
AND TO MAKE TEACHERS PROUD!**

HOW TO USE
"GOOD FOR YOUR CLASS!"

This section contains motivational awards to encourage and reward students as well as to make teachers proud and establish positive relations. There are three kinds of awards:

Quiet Class Awards

Give these awards to classes that are well-mannered in the library/media center.

Book Return Awards

Give these awards when everyone in a class returns his or her books on library day.

Neat 'N Tidy Awards

Give these awards to classes that leave the library neat 'n tidy.

Here are some helpful hints to establish a successful award system:

- Have teachers post their awards on the outsides of their classroom doors for other classes and school visitors to see.
- Keep track of which class has the most awards by posting incentive charts on the library bulletin board.
- Announce weekly winners in the library newsletter. (See "Getting The Word Out!")
- Give a treat to the class having the most awards at the end of the year.

I COULD GET **A-COSTUMED** TO THIS!

Thank you, _____, for returning all your books on _____.

Thanks a **HEAP**, **PILGRIMS!**

for returning all your books on _____.

BOOK RETURN AWARD

BOOT-IFUL JOB!

Thanks, _____, for returning all your books on _____.

BOOK RETURN AWARD

I'M HEARTENED

Thank you, _____, for returning all your books on _____.

BOOK RETURN AWARD

BOOK RETURN AWARD

IT HAS HOP-PENED !!

Thank you, _____, for returning all your books on _____.

How TIMELY of you!

Thank you, _____, for returning all your books on _____.

BOOK RETURN AWARD

Simply De-vine!

Thank you, _____,
for minding your
media center/library
manners and being
especially quiet on
_____ .

QUIET CLASS AWARD

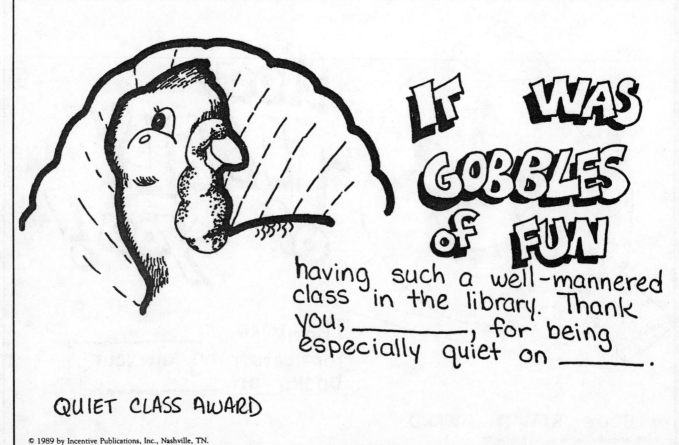

IT WAS GOBBLES of FUN

having such a well-mannered
class in the library. Thank
you, _____, for being
especially quiet on _____ .

QUIET CLASS AWARD

IT'S A TREAT!

having such a quiet class in the library!

Thank you, _____,
for minding your media center/library manners on

_____.

QUIET CLASS AWARD

QUIET CLASS AWARD

HEART-LY HEARD ANY NOISE!

(and I LOVE IT)

Thank you, _____, for especially minding your media center/library manners on _____.

QUIET CLASS AWARD

I WAS ALL EARS...

BUT I DIDN'T HEAR ANY NOISE!

Thank you, _____, for especially minding your media center/library manners on _____.

QUIET CLASS AWARD

SUPER KIDS!

Thank you, _____, for especially minding your media center/ library manners on _____.

WHO GHOST TO THE LIBRARY and leaves it NEAT 'N TIDY? You did on _____. Thanks!

YOU FEATHERED YOUR CAPS, PILGRIMS !!! Thanks for leaving the library NEAT 'N TIDY on _____.

I'm glad you're HUNG UP on being NEAT 'N TIDY! Great job on _____!

NEAT 'N TIDY AWARD

YOU DIDN'T MISS A BEAT! Thanks for leaving the library NEAT 'N TIDY on _____.

NEAT 'N TIDY AWARD

YOU WERE **GOOD EGGS** and left the library NEAT 'N TIDY on _____. You should **BASK**-in-**ET!**

NEAT 'N TIDY AWARD

NEAT 'N TIDY AWARD

IT'S NEAT when you're **NEAT!** Thanks for leaving the library NEAT 'N TIDY on _____.

WHAT A CLASS ACT!

CONGRATULATIONS, _____
YOUR CLASS RECEIVED THE MOST
_____ AWARDS THIS YEAR.

THANK YOU FOR YOUR SUPPORT
AND ENCOURAGEMENT.

'SPECIALLY FOR YOU!

NOTICES AND CARDS FOR
TEACHERS AND STUDENTS

HOW TO USE
"SPECIALLY FOR YOU!"

Special Occasion Notices

These attractive special occasion notices will help you to notify teachers and their students of special celebrations, library orientation, special programs, book fairs, open house, and a hardware training seminar!

Cards

These specially designed cards for open house and many holidays will help you to strengthen relations and good will.

* Open House

Cut out the open house card sections on page 72 and insert a brad through the holes. Fill in the blanks with the appropriate information.

* Halloween, Thanksgiving, and Christmas

Follow these instructions to make the cards on pages 73 - 78:

1. Tear out the page or make a two-sided photocopy with side A on one side and side B on the other. If your copy machine does not have this capability, make a copy of each side and glue the copies together as shown.
2. Fold the card along the dotted lines.
3. Cut out the image if you wish.

 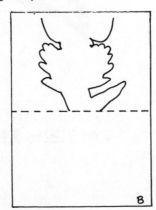   

* Valentine's Day

Cut out the broken heart halves and the whole heart on page 79. Insert a brad through the holes so that the whole heart is behind the broken heart halves. When the broken heart halves are pulled apart, the message shows.

* Easter

Cut out the egg halves on page 80 and insert a brad through the holes. Glue the "message" behind section B.

WE'RE CELEBRATING

IN THE LIBRARY

Event: _____

Date(s): _____ Time(s): _____

_____ _____

LIBRARY ORIENTATION — a FAN-TASTIC

way to discover what your library has to offer!

Date: _____

Time: _____

The movie/special program, _____, will air closed circuit on _____ at _____, channel ___. ENJOY!

...pssst! Giving you FAIR warning! BOOK FAIR
Date(s): _____
Time(s): _____
Your scheduled visit:
_____

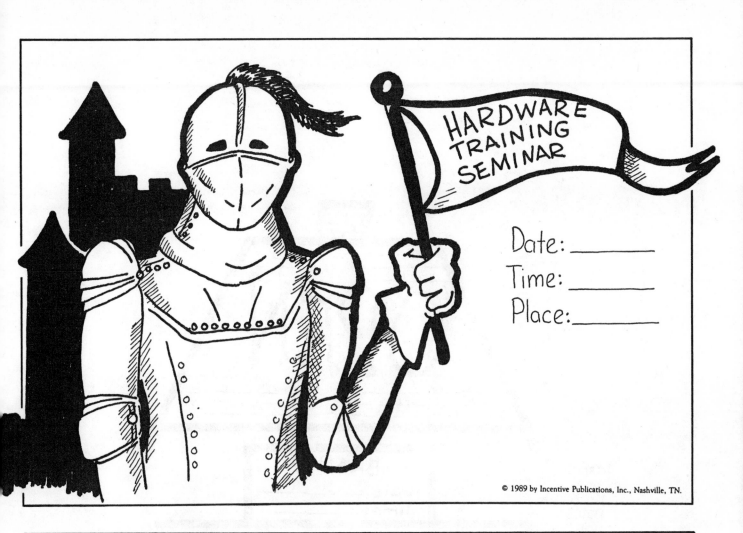

HARDWARE TRAINING SEMINAR

Date: _____
Time: _____
Place: _____

OPEN HOUSE in the LIBRARY!

Date: _____
Time: _____

Insert
brad
through
holes

LIBRARY!
Date:_____
Time:_____

A.

IS SPECIAL
???
ALL OF YOU!
HAPPY
HALLOWEEN
FROM YOUR LIBRARY

you this card is the
thing to do . . .

**happy
Thanksgiving**

from your
library!

A.

© 1989 by Incentive Publications, Inc., Nashville, TN.

NOT SENDING
HOLIDAY
GREETINGS
from the
LIBRARY!

B.

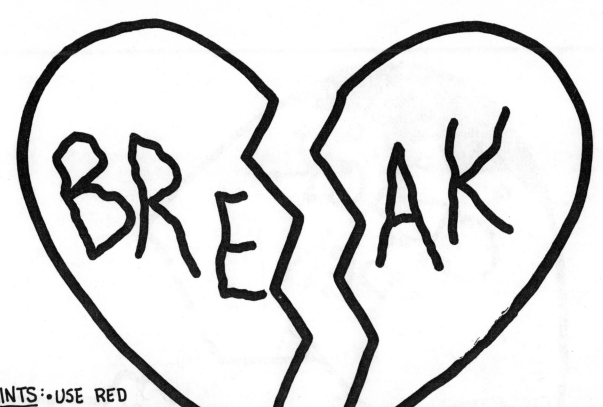

HINTS: • USE RED CONSTRUCTION PAPER.
• WRITE "BREAK" WITH GLUE, COVER WITH GLITTER AND SHAKE TO REMOVE EXCESS.

OPEN VALENTINE GREETINGS FROM THE... LIBRARY!

PLACE WHOLE HEART BEHIND HEART HALVES. INSERT ONE BRAD THROUGH ALL 3 HOLES. MESSAGE APPEARS WHEN HALVES ARE PULLED APART.